Mexico is the United States' southern neig it is referred to as Estados Unidos M ... translates as United Mexican States. Spanish is Mexico's official language, as Spain dominated the country for 300 years. In the 1500s, Spanish conquistadors came to Mexico. The conquistadors destroyed the Aztec empire in Mexico. Spain ruled Mexico until 1821 when it declared independence.

Mexico City is the country's capital and the country's most populous city. This city is now home to more than 21.7 million people. The Aztec Empire's capital, now known as Mexico City, was established where the modern city now stands. The city's initial structures made extensive use of stone from the Aztec capital. It's now a bustling metropolis with many skyscrapers and broad tree-lined boulevards.

Mexico City, the country's most populous city, has a rich history and culture. Mexico City offers delicious food, ancient Aztec ruins, and world-class hotels at a reasonable price. If you want to splash out, the Avenida Presidente Masaryk in Polanco has many high-end shops. The Palace of Fine Arts and the Basilica of Our Lady of Guadalupe are must-see cultural attractions. A food tour is an ideal way to see the city while eating your way through it.

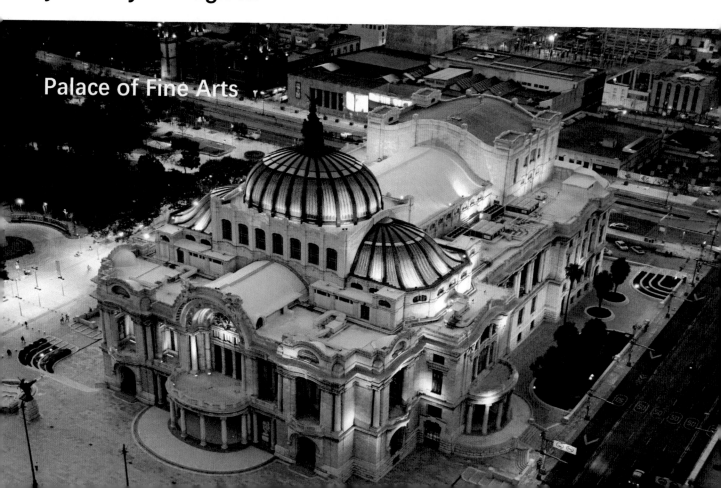

Palace of Fine Arts

The pristine white sands and crystal-clear waters of Mexico's coasts captivate tourists year after year. Among Mexico's most popular holiday destinations are Acapulco, Mazatlan, and Puerto Vallarta. The Yucatán Peninsula in southeastern Mexico is also home to a number of well-known hotels and resorts. It's no secret that Mexico is a popular vacation destination.

Mexico has breathtaking scenery. Northcentral Mexico appears to be the setting for a cowboy movie. The bone-dry desert is covered in sagebrush and is cut by deep canyons. Tropical forests abound in southern Mexico. Central Mexico is a high plateau surrounded by snowcapped mountains on both sides. Active volcanoes, such as Popocatépetl, occasionally spew smoke into the sky.

Popocatépetl Volcano

Many visitors to Mexico come to see the ruins of ancient civilizations. Long before Europeans arrived, Native Americans such as the Olmec, Zapotec, Maya, Toltec, and Aztec developed civilizations in Mexico. They built magnificent cities, complete with massive stone pyramids and other religious structures.

Mexico's culture is diverse, bright, and colorful, impacted by ancient civilizations such as the Aztec and Maya and European invasions. It is a one-of-a-kind civilization that is perhaps one of the most fascinating in the world.

The Maya had a sophisticated culture. They were gifted in mathematics. They knew a lot about the stars. They devised a complex and precise calendar. They used a writing system that is no longer understandable.

The Aztecs were in charge of the last great Native American kingdom. They built a magnificent city called Tenochtitlán. The Aztecs had a religion in which people were sacrificed. Spanish explorer Cortés and his small army wiped out the Aztec Empire in 1520, which led to a Spanish empire in Mexico.

In 1861, Benito Juárez was elected President of Mexico. Later that year, European countries invaded Mexico in order to recover money due to them by Mexico. Mexico overcame French forces in a conflict that is commemorated on the Cinco de Mayo celebration today. France, on the other hand, took control in 1864 and reigned until 1867.

Between 1810 and 1815, Mexicans revolted against Spanish control. Mexico later gained its independence from Spain in 1821. Until 1823, Mexico was ruled by a monarchy.

Independence Angel

The Day of the Dead is perhaps the first thing that springs to mind when you think of Mexican yearly events. After all, this historic, spiritual, and very significant annual practice honoring the deceased by celebrating their life is uniquely Mexican and honored across the country.

Mariachi is a type of regional Mexican music that has existed since at least the 18th century and has evolved over time in the countryside of various regions of western Mexico. This musical style has grown in popularity outside of Mexico. UNESCO even designated mariachi as part of the Intangible Cultural Heritage of Humanity in 2011.

Throughout Mexico, folk dance is a popular pastime. One of Mexico's most well-known dances, the Jarabe Tapatio (Mexican Hat Dance), can be considered the country's unofficial national dance. The dancing is centered on a sombrero and is meant to commemorate courtship.

When the Spanish conquerors arrived in Mexico in 1519, the Aztecs ruled much of the country. The Aztec Empire had been conquered by the Spanish conqueror Hernán Cortés and his forces by 1521. New Spain was the Spanish name for Mexico at that point. A large number of indigenous peoples were converted to Christianity by the Spanish. They also forced the indigenous people to labor in mines and plantations

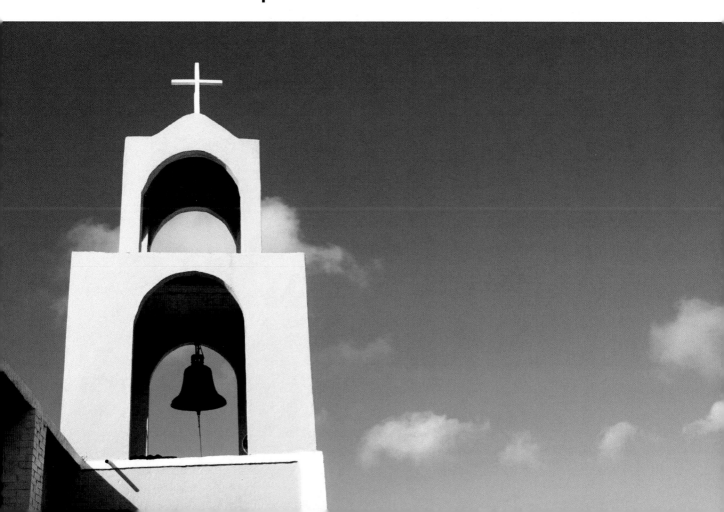

In 1833, General Antonio López de Santa Anna was elected President of Mexico. He ran into trouble in Texas, which was then part of Mexico. The people of Texas revolted against Mexican rule in 1836. Santa Anna attempted but failed to put an end to the rebellion. Texas was annexed by the United States in 1845. This resulted in the Mexican War, a conflict between Mexico and the United States. Mexico was defeated in the war in 1848. It ceded a large portion of its territory to the United States.

Texas state flag

Many Mexicans still work as farmers, even though agriculture is no longer a large part of the economy. Sugarcane, corn, fruits, vegetables, and beans are among the most important crops. Pigs and cattle comprise the bulk of the country's livestock herd. As well as providing jobs, logging and fishing contribute to the local economy.

Mexico's economy relies heavily on services such as transportation, education, and health care. It's no secret that tourism is a pillar industry in Mexico. Millions of people flock to Mexico each year to enjoy its resorts and ancient sites.

Beach in Cancun

Chichen Itza is one of Mexico's most important archaeological sites. Itza, the so-called water sorcerers, built the city in the 5th century AD, and it remains a revered Mayan pilgrimage site. As one of the most prominent pre-Hispanic cities in Mexico, Chichen Itza remains a popular tourist destination.

In this UNESCO World Heritage-listed city, colonial buildings, bustling plazas, and colorful homes are everywhere you look. If you're looking for an adventure, Guanajuato's underground streets and tunnels can be explored on a walking tour or at your own pace. It's an excellent place to pick up a souvenir or some food after exploring the city's cobblestone streets and admiring its beautiful architecture. When the Festival Internacional Cervantino takes place in October, it's a great time to visit for art lovers.

Because of its Mayan ruins and its proximity to the water, Tulum is a popular destination for history buffs and those who love the outdoors. Hotels of all sizes can be found in the Riviera Maya area, from small boutique hotels and wellness retreats to all-inclusive hotels and beachfront villas.

Ruins in Tulum

Travelers will be able to pick and choose the vacation that best suits them. No matter where you stay, the Yucatan Peninsula's unique underwater caves, such as the cenotes and the beach, are all just a short walk away.

Cenote diving

Foodies can sample everything from tacos and tostadas to sushi and fresh seafood in Playa del Carmen, which also has a thriving bar scene. In addition, the Riviera Maya's soft sand blanketing its beaches and its breathtaking shoreline views entice vacationers to this destination. Golf courses and cenotes are both within biking distance for those looking to cool off during their stay.

Travelers from the United States flock to Cancun for its sandy beaches, nightclubs, and all-inclusive resorts in the spring. However, the city is close to lush jungles, tranquil cenotes, and an impressive network of caverns, making it a great destination for outdoor lovers. In addition, the downtown area offers a wide variety of cheap and tasty street food options. Visiting in the fall or winter is the best time of year to see this city at its most peaceful.

Coral reefs and cruise ships are Cozumel's main attractions. Water sports and laid-back beaches make this destination a popular choice for vacationers. Kayaks, paddleboards, and snorkeling gear are available from a wide variety of outfitters and resorts. However, Cozumel is a great place to learn about Mayan culture and unwind on the beach while reading a good book. Visit the Mayan ruins at San Gervasio Archaeological Zone for a taste of history.

A trip to Puebla will provide you with a memorable experience full of local flavor. Located about 86 miles southeast of Mexico City, this colonial city is known for its stunning Talavera pottery and its sweet and spiciness cuisine, which are the city's main attractions.

Chiles en nogada and mole poblano are two must-try dishes for visitors to the city of Poblano, Mexico. Listen to live music at Callejón de los Sapos when the sun goes down.

Chiles en nogada

mole poblano

Learn about Mexican culture firsthand by visiting this colonial city in southern Mexico. Oaxaca, perched atop the Sierra Madre del Sur mountain range at an elevation of over 5,000 feet, is a great place to learn about indigenous culture, browse colorful markets, and eat delectable local cuisine. The 16th-century Templo de Santo Domingo church, which served as a military barracks for a time, and the well-preserved ruins of Monte Albán are notable cultural landmarks.

Huatulco, a coastal town in the state of Oaxaca, boasts nine bays and 36 beaches. The town's visitor accommodations are of a high standard without being ostentatious, and environmental preservation is a top priority. Consequently, buildings are limited to six stories in height and the lush natural landscape is preserved. snorkeling and eco-tours are two of the most popular ways to spend a day out. Spend your days relaxing on the beach and sampling the town's variety of seaside bars and restaurants if you'd rather take it easy.

Zacatecas is a great place to escape the crowds and get a taste of real Mexico. As a former silver mining hotspot, this colonial city is filled with historical and cultural landmarks like the Museo Pedro Coronel and the Mina El Edén, which houses a rock and mineral museum from the 16th century. Take a cable car ride to the top of Cerro de la Bufa, which offers stunning city views.

Tourists flock to Puerto Vallarta in search of beautiful beaches and regional cuisine. Apart from this, the town's picturesque location on Mexico's western coast and landmarks like the Church of Our Lady of Guadalupe and Los Arcos National Marine Park set it apart from other tourist traps – and make for great photo ops. Whale-watching tours and tequila tastings are just some of the activities available to visitors.

Some of Mexico's most luxurious hotels and world-class golf courses can be found in Cabo San Lucas, the Baja peninsula's party capital. Only a few stretches of sand are suitable for swimming due to the strong undercurrents and steep ocean floor drop-offs, but the beaches themselves are stunning. If you're looking for a break from Cabo's crowded beaches and raucous nightlife, consider staying in San José del Cabo, which is just a short drive away.

Arch of Cabo San Lucas

Mérida's vibrant cultural heritage is on display at every turn as Yucatan's capital city. The city's main street, Paseo de Montejo, is lined with stately white stone mansions, and the lively Sunday markets here offer a taste of old Mexico.

As far as Mayan ruins go, you're in luck. There are a couple of archaeological sites within a short distance. Museum-goers laud the city's El Gran Museo del Mundo Maya de Mérida, as well as the city's art galleries and public murals. Travelers can choose from a variety of charming boutique hotels for their vacation.

El Gran Museo del Mundo Maya de Mérida

Walking around San Miguel de Allende, you might think you've stepped back in time. Visit this city to see how colonial architecture coexists peacefully with modern art galleries and retail establishments. Visit the Parroquia de San Miguel Arcángel, one of San Miguel de Allende's beloved landmarks, and its open-air markets. You should also be prepared to change your daily schedule, as something is bound to be going on during your stay. Music festivals and religious holidays are among the city's many year-round celebrations.

With its Mayan culture and colonial architecture mingled, San Cristóbal de las Casas, Mexico's southernmost state, is a fascinating mix of urban and rural. Visit the Centro de Textiles del Mundo Maya and the Asociación Cultural Na Bolom while you're in the city center to learn more about the region's indigenous cultures and their enduring traditions.